Reinvent Yourself.

Discover The Brilliance Within &

Create Infinite Possibilities

Adaobi Onyekweli

Title: Reinvent Yourself
Subtitle: Discover The Brilliance Within & Create Infinite Possibilities

ISBN: 9781097605644

Book Design & Book Writing, Coaching & Publishing done by:
Lily Patrascu
Brand for Speakers
www.brandforspeakers.com

TABLE OF CONTENTS

Praise For The Book

"*Life is a gift, a privilege we only get to experience once! We take this gift for granted. We forget that we don't have this body forever. It's more like a rental for a short short time and one day we must return it as the rental has expired. In her book Adaobi shares her story and her fight to stay alive against all odds. She reminds us that life is indeed worth fighting for and we must ensure that we live each day with no regrets and take nothing for granted as indeed every experience is a pure privilege. She shares advice for each of us and reminds us that it's never too late to make changes to improve our daily lives so we can create the quality of life with more awareness and gratitude. She reminds us of how the quality of our life truly makes a difference not only for ourselves but also for those around us who love us and value the journey of living life with us as part of their lives.*"
Martina Coogan, CEO of The Mystery School Europe, www.MartinaCoogan.com

"After listening to Adaobi's incredible story of triumph through adversity, of never giving up, and the strength of the human spirit, I have never felt so humbled, inspired and uplifted by the wonderful human being that she is.

Adaobi's extraordinary journey, is a gift for us all to realise that it's never too late to set a goal, and achieve your dreams in life. The powerful lessons that Adaobi will teach you will empower you with hope, self belief, gratitude and show you how to reach the greatness within you.

"Reinvent Yourself" is a shining light for us all to find our true calling and purpose...this book will change your life."

Steve Frew
Scotland's First Gymnastics Commonwealth Games Gold Medallist

"Adaobi is a woman of substance, a woman who has looked death in the face and conquered it. Her resilience is second to none and she is always upbeat about life. She is incredibly nice and a fighter. She is a brilliant communicator, her attention to details is remarkable. She speaks from the heart. Truly, she is a woman of great courage. I admire her tenacity to want to touch lives and show people how to reinvent themselves. Keep inspiring us all."

Jimmy Asuni, Motivational Speaker, Author of the book "Dare To Be Imperfect"

"Adaobi's book is very well done. The minute I started reading it, I was completely drawn to a wonderful and empowering story. Her book is made so clearly and easy to understand. I was very pleasantly surprised with the level of detail about her life transformation. She has a handful of excellent, well thought out stories. She has carefully created the Reinvention Mastery Program that will surely help those who need a wake up call. I strongly recommend to get your hands on this book. She emphasised the importance and the benefits of how we should live our lives to the fullest, and that we must do the best we can – because everything else is uncertain, for the sake of the one life that has been given to us and also

for people around us. It delivers a very powerful message."
Teuta Avdyli, Empowerment Speaker, Author of the book "Born To Stand Out, Not To Fit In"

"What I loved about Reinvent Yourself is the incredible inspiring and gripping story of survival of Adaobi against all odds, whose message is that it is not too late for second chances, and it is never too late to start living the life you really want to live."
Harry Sardinas, Empowerment, Public Speaking and Leadership Coach, Author, www.SpeakersAreLeaders.com

"Adaobi's story will leave you inspired & remind you that life is a precious gift which should never be taken for granted. It reminds you how quickly it can change & how it's never too late to make huge life changes no matter what your age or background. Uplifting, inspiring & life-affirming. Thank you Adaobi."
Ben Brophy, TheONlineVideoAcademy.com & TheInternetBusinessSchool.com

"A real human story touching every aspect of our creation where service to others played havoc on the HEART. 'Reinvent Yourself' gives credence to a new creation where the HEART takes control and designs the best version of YOU. What I found fascinating was the simplicity of the steps to happiness and a wish filled life the second time around. Adaobi's story is a must for humanity, health institutions like WHO, schools, workplaces globally."
Antonetta Fernandes,
www.AntonettaFernandes.co.uk

"Reading this book is a real eye-opener about life processes and how we can live and prosper in this "given life". I will definitely recommend this book."
Aruere Harriet Bukata, Director,
Oak Solicitors Limited, London

"I am amazed at how the author Adaobi has the

courage to share her experience before her illness and after with the world. She has really empowered me and giving me an insight into why we should live in the moment. This book delivers the most practical and straightforward tutorial I have ever read to make me more focused."
Apostle Ada Nwachukwu, CEO, Tina Talk Show

"This book, which you will find difficult to stop reading once you've started is a real experience of Adaobi, who constantly lives for others. I would greatly recommend it since it is coming from a real life physical and emotional survivor."
Augustine Onyekweli

"This is an awesome and inspirational book. A must read to enrich one's life and discover your purpose. Adaobi is a good friend of more than 10 years through our journey in Mary kay Cosmetics. I provided support to her through her journey both emotionally and as an informal mentor. I witnessed part of her journey and I know this book will inspire

anyone who dares to read it, to "discover who you are"."

Dr Oluwatoyin Magbagbeola,
MaryKay.co.uk/tmagbagbeola

"Words fail to express how much I glorify God for Adaobi's Life. It was a moment in time that we met at a charity workshop and after Adaobi shared her story, I was speechless for the rest of the day. Her experience and determination to live again is inspiring.

I was privileged to accompany her to the hospital for follow up analysis and as the doctors reiterated all the medical issues Adaobi had gone through, I could not but thank God for her life.
This book will make very real and strong positive impact on anyone who cares to learn about her situation. I thank God to have met her. I pray that all those who read her book will feel inspired to help others. God bless you Adaobi."

Jackie Oni, Director,
God's Children Empowered Ltd (Charity),
GodschildrenEmpowered.com

"Adaobi is a living testimony of God's design and purpose for creation. The life after death reality is brought to the fore in a manner that is indisputable. The lesson is for all mankind irrespective of religion. The book is a must read!"
Professor Chris Ugolo, Professor of African Dance, University of Benin, Benin, Nigeria.

"Adaobi's book is incredible as only very few will testify to this. I now believe we are on a long journey and Mother Earth is just a transit to further evolution the end point which we may never know. What a vivid account and brilliance coupled with accuracy."
Dr Matthew Onyekweli

"It's time to 'Reinvent Yourself'. This inspiring book written by one of the most beautiful women walking on planet Earth, is a must read. She had been through it all, and she has refused to give up *on her dreams. This book will provoke you to step out of your comfort zone, and make those necessary changes that would positively transform your life. I was privileged to interview Ms Onyekweli for our magazine after she came out of COMA. Get inspired by reading this book."*

Lady Anita Duckworth-Bradshaw,
Powerhouse Global Propagator,
PowerHouseGlobalmag.com,
PowerHouseGlobalwomen.com

"This book is a riveting account of one person's experience during a very serious illness and surviving it to share the captivating and compelling story."

Louis Onyekweli

You Can't Turn Back Time.

LIVE IN

THE

MOMENT.

Foreword By Harry Sardinas, Empowerment, Public Speaking and Leadership Coach

Reinvent Yourself *is the story of a mother who wasn't living her true purpose in life and, as a result, she was all of a sudden struck with a wake-up call.*

Imagine having plans with your children, being about to spend Christmas with them, and all of a sudden having to stop because you are no longer living.

I don't know why you picked up this book, but I do know everything in life happens for a reason.

Perhaps it is time for you to have a wake-up call – to find your own purpose in life, or perhaps it is time to look at your own life from a different perspective.

As an empowerment, public speaking and leadership coach, my role is to encourage anyone wanting more out of life.

I empower ordinary people to create extraordinary results by activating the power they have within, through overcoming the fear of speaking, which enables them to find their voice, and create a ripple effect of transformation in the world. I do this with the Speakers Are Leaders international speaking and leadership programme that has so far trained more than 10,000 people internationally, in the UK, Singapore, Peru and Mexico, to gain the confidence to speak and monetize their knowledge.

I was inspired to read Adaobi's story, because she went through a moment of decision-making. She could have given up – but she chose to fight to stay alive, so she could fulfil her destiny. I believe it is never too late to be who you might have been.

Adaobi reinvented herself and recreated her story. She didn't want her story to end. She wanted to inspire women – in particular, young mothers – and people in general to take control of their own life and finally start living their full potential.

How about you? Perhaps you are ready to overcome the fear of truly living. Perhaps you are ready to LIVE every moment fully. Perhaps you are ready to appreciate every moment with your family. This book will inspire you to access your best version of yourself, come out of the routine and feel excited about living.

I encourage you to absorb every word, reinvent yourself, and I hope to meet you someday!

Harry Sardinas
www.SpeakersAreLeaders.com

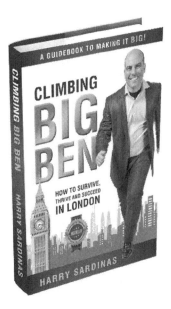

NEVER TAKE TIME FOR GRANTED.

Live Today, Instead Of Wasting Time Regretting Yesterday.

About The Book

Imagine going about your daily life and all of a sudden getting a wake-up call out of the blue.

Reinvent Yourself is based on the Reinvention Mastery Programme, which offers a blueprint for you to find your purpose, ignite your passion, find the joy and excitement in your life so you can fulfil your destiny, and transform your life through a series of simple steps.

It was created based on the experience of a young mother existing between life and death, fighting for her life after having five heart attacks in four days which left her brain dead for more than one month. The doctors gave her less than a 0.1% chance of survival – and were ready to switch off her life support several times.

Through a twist of fate, she managed to wake up in the nick of time and recreate her life, after surviving multiple organ failures and having taken several medicines over the course of a year.

Discover how she managed to reinvent herself and her life, and how you can do it, too.

She experienced a near-death tragedy which left her in a coma fighting for her life for months. During that time, she experienced a spiritual awakening which shifted her entire perspective on life.

Adaobi created a Reinvention Mastery Programme, which is a series of simple habits and rituals that will enable you to empower yourself to see the brilliance within and discover the endless possibilities in your life.

To Live Is To

ENJOY

EVERY

SINGLE

MOMENT IN

YOUR LIFE.

About The Author
My Story

Ever since I was young, I had a big dream of becoming an international public speaker. I knew I was destined for greatness. I could see very clearly, in my mind, huge crowds listening very carefully and absorbing every word I spoke, clapping, cheering, taking notes, learning and implementing my words of wisdom.

However, whilst living in Nigeria, the reality was very different. I was always surrounded by people who seemed to discourage any thought of greatness I had.

In fact, the bigger the dreams I had for myself, the more they discouraged me.

"You can't do this", "You can't do that", "You will never be able to do this", "Who do you think you are?", "You don't have the money", "You don't have the knowledge", "Women aren't supposed to do this" – those were the words I kept hearing over and over – from people who clearly meant well but had no idea what the impact would be on me.

As I grew up, I became more and more hopeless and started having thoughts of killing myself. After all, what was the point of living, if I couldn't be who I was meant to become?

I started giving up on myself, on my hopes and dreams of someday becoming an inspiring speaker.

I eventually started fitting in and got married; I pushed my dreams to the side.

I started off as an early morning cleaner, washing toilets at McDonald's in Oxford Circus for two years. Luck seemed to strike when I started working in a William Hill betting shop, but it ended soon enough when the shop was robbed two years later.
After several jobs in IT support for several banks, I had two great children and started promoting healthy living. I was looking for ways to create flexible income based around looking after the children.

If you looked at my life as an outsider, you would have been struck by my apparent "picture perfect" life and perhaps you would have envied me. "She has it all," you would have said, looking at the nice clothes, the curvy body, the loving husband, the gorgeous healthy children, the house, the flexible working.

The truth was that I felt a deep void in my life. I was spiritually void, disconnected from everything that mattered.

I was resigned about my life; I was resigned about my marriage. I was resigned about my job and the income I was hardly creating. I was resigned about shouting at my kids every time they created mess in the house or weren't behaving well. I was resigned about how I looked, the food I ate, the promises I made to people. I was resigned about not fulfilling my hopes and dreams. I was resigned about the house I was living in. I had let myself down. "This is not my life," I kept saying to myself. "This is not a life worth living."

What kind of life was I providing for my children? What kind of life was I living? I was always so stressed out, so OVERWHELMED. So many things to do, so little time. There had to be perfection. I had to have control and yet it felt like I had lost control of everything. Nothing was really working. I was pretending I was okay. I was pretending I wasn't stressed, I was pretending I wasn't overwhelmed. I was pretending the world was swirling around my finger.

One day it dawned on me I had given up on LIVING a life of true purpose.

I was lost. I stopped believing in myself.

I started believing the stories others told me – after all, it was true I was not worth it. It was true that I really could not achieve anything in my life. I could not understand **why** was this happening to ME.

People frequently needed my help. As they were asking, I was there for them. Pleasing people seemed to be my full-time job.

I was preaching healthy living, teaching people how to prevent heart attacks and diabetes, yet I was not always eating well. I felt inauthentic. I was there for everyone BUT MYSELF.

And then the unexpected happened.

It was a very NORMAL day on the 24th of December 2017 which changed my life forever. It was a crucial day that made me realise how precious was the gift of life.

The morning of 24th December 2017 was no different from any other. The Christmas spirit surrounded everything. Everyone around was rushing, rushing ... getting anxious over last minute presents, waiting in endless traffic jams, arguing over whose turn it was to pick up the children ... so much to do, so little time ...

Luckily, everybody I knew was taken care of since I had delivered all the presents for everyone way in advance.

As I took a quick glance at my cousin, who was sporadically stuffing her clothes into a small suitcase, I had a fleeting premonition about something terrible that was going to unfold in the next two minutes.
All I can remember is an unexpected feeling of an overwhelming foreboding, followed by sudden breathlessness.
As I hit the floor, everything around me seemed to swirl fast, faster, even faster ... at whirlwind speed.

Running out of breath, I called my cousin Rita and my son, Tosin, for help. My desperate cry for help seemed to travel in sloooooow, SLOW motion ... Nothing seemed to matter anymore. My entire life seemed to flash in front of my eyes in a split second. Then 9 – 9 – 9 ... my cousin dialled.

Within seconds, I lost consciousness.

I seemed to be dreaming. An immediate feeling of peace seemed to set in.

I felt like I was travelling – or floating above many countries I had never seen before – whilst attached to the bed.

It seemed I was in a surreal place. Many relatives that had been dead for a long time were asking me to go through a door full of light.

The paramedics barged in with trepidation. Whilst my children and my cousin were paralysed with fear, the ambulance crew desperately tried with all their heart and soul, but could not resuscitate me. I suffered five cardiac arrests in the next four days and I was immediately placed in an induced coma. I was fighting between life and death.

Whilst in the coma I developed multiple life-threatening conditions: blood clots, multiple organ failure, multiple pulmonary embolisms, liver haematoma, biliary sepsis. Within days, I was declared brain dead. Multiple doctors were fighting to keep me alive. After a month of trying to bring me back to life, they gave up.

My family was informed they would need to sign a paper to allow the doctors to switch off my life support.

As the doctors were informing my family, I was begging God to let me live. I said: "God, please, please give me another chance. I don't want to die now. What will happen to my children? What will happen to my family? I haven't lived my life yet. Let me live, God, and I promise this time I will do better. I promise, God, this time, if you let me live, I will come back to the world to fulfil my destiny."

I woke up more than one month later, on the 30th January 2018. Later on, I found out what had happened to me.

As I came back to life, I was afraid of the doctors. There was so much I could not do for many months on end.

I was like a vegetable; this time, I knew, however, I was going to do what was necessary to live my destiny, to reinvent myself, to be an author and a speaker, to fulfil my full potential and, most importantly, to help others to fulfil their potential, too.

I had made a promise to God I was going to fulfil my destiny and I was going to transmit to the world the big message that God had asked me to send to humanity — which was to LIVE every moment, to find and live your purpose and to be grateful. We are all on Earth to fulfil a purpose; it is your duty to figure out what it is and to help as many people as possible in the process.

I really now believe we are all, to some extent, not fulfilling our full potential — we are capable of so much more. In fact, sometimes less is more.

Simplicity, and reducing overwhelm to let in some key things that need to be accomplished, could make us feel happier, more connected to who we really are. Whilst trying to do more, we are overwhelmed with information, stuff to do.

We are forgetting who we really are, what we love, the fun, the spiritual connection. My mission is to help you discover your passion, your joy of living — because when you do that, and you find the strength and the power to live the life you are capable of living, then you will be happy and you will have fulfilled your dreams. Many people are amazed and ask if I had fully recovered to the point of normality. When you read this book, you will be able to see the miracle of God in action.

Read on, and you will discover the full story.

Be GRATEFUL,

APPRECIATE The Little Things In Life.

Note To The Reader

Dear Reader,
Imagine coming home one day and everything you planned to do is cancelled because you simply don't exist anymore. Your heart stopped out of the blue in the face of too much stress.

I don't want this to happen to you. In fact, the opposite. I want you to rejoice and cherish every moment in your life because time is limited. We only think about what we need to do and get trapped into the daily routine and forget to take time for ourselves, to meditate, to listen to what we really want. We ignore all the signs.

If you were to take only one thing out of this book, it should be this: live your life, not your parents' life, not your family's life, not what other people tell you that you should be doing. Choose to live your own life, without regrets.

I have lived a life of procrastination and not taking life seriously. I had often neglected my own needs whilst focusing on dealing with others' demands. This obviously affected my self-esteem greatly. I was not aware of the negative vibration which played an active role in my daily personal behaviour.

I have realised that since my return to life, my focus has changed a great deal. I am more aware of my own personal needs. Things that used to bother me no longer matter to me. Forgiveness has become a daily practice (both personally and towards others).

It's a whole new world for me. I would want you to know that there's hope in every new day. You should put away negativity due to the adverse effect on your personal health. You should enjoy life to the fullest and get away from stress.

My overall suggestion is to USE YOUR GIFTS TO ILLUMINATE THE DARKNESS IN YOUR WORLD. My biggest goal is to get my story out to the world through various media, and for my story to serve as a positive reflection so you, too, can reinvent yourself.

In Life,
YOU DON'T GET THE SAME MOMENT TWICE.
Cherish Every Single One.

Who Should Read This Book?

There are several groups of people who should read this book right now: millionaires, entrepreneurs, business leaders, church leaders, stay at home mums and any ordinary people who are looking for something bigger in their life.

Who This Is For?

Business Executives. To be more specific, this is for business executives, people that employ others, such as HR, since they are the ones that hire and fire staff.

They're under a lot of stress.

Anyone who's stressed out can benefit from it, but my focus is on high-flyers and the people at the top, like senior executives.

We will be able to easily work together, because I have worked there.

Single Mums. Another interest I have is in single mothers. Why? Because society undervalues single mothers.

Single mothers are very productive, but they are not being recognised.

With the kind of things they're going through, I can actually see the pattern of it all and provide guidance.

Couples. I believe I can help couples who have marital problems.

Young People. My other interest is young people in their twenties, so that they can follow the right path before they turn forty.

Those who may find it beneficial are those who have to make decisions that impact daily livelihood, especially stress-related ones.

The more clarity you have in your life, the more balanced you begin to feel. The consequence of this is the daily abundance that you feel, improved health and a sense of fulfilment.

Steve Jobs once said that remembering that you are going to die was the best way he knew to avoid the trap of thinking you have something to lose. You are already naked. There is no reason not to follow your heart.

When I read that quote, it made me begin a

process that I have come to call the Miracle Golden Evening Ritual. This is because a golden day begins with a simple ritual that will always lead to your golden day. I would love it if you implemented the Miracle Golden Evening Ritual into your day as I am confident it will lead to great results.

If You Aren't Who You Want To Be,

DON'T

QUIT.

It's Time To Reinvent Yourself.

Acknowledgements & Gratitude

First and foremost, I thank God for giving me a second chance to live again.

I would like to show my sincere gratitude to my mother, Grace Ulo Onyekweli for bringing me into this world. My gratitude also extends to my late father, Christopher Ozegbe Onyekweli.

To my siblings, for always believing and encouraging me in whatever I set out to do. Thank you for making me become the person I am today. You all have my greatest respect: Omogo Adiasor, Evelyn Onyekweli, Augustine Onyekweli, Dr Matthew Onyekweli, Christopher Onyekweli and John Olisa Onyekweli. You guys continually inspire me and make me proud.

To my amazing and awesome godchildren - Maria Changwareza (aka MJ, Junior) and Israel Darlington.

While I was being hospitalised, I received a lot of emotional support from my uncle, Retired Major-General Philip Osoloka Onyekweli and also from John Onyekweli, Louis Onyekweli and Mrs Felicia Olanrewaju, who all helped my reality.

To all my incredible cousins, Louis Onyekweli, Angela Ihezie, Obiora Onyekweli, Rita Adaobi Onyekweli, Valentine Onyekweli and Pamela Anomneze (she was invited to Prince Harry and Meghan's wedding ceremony).

My amazing Sister in-laws Franca and Rosemary Onyekweli whose prayers were unrelentless.

To some of my inspiring and loyal friends whom I am blessed to have in my life: Adwoa Asomani, Benedict Kemayou, Emma Kemevor, Pep Graham-Afari, Dupe Balogun. "You all know who you are!"

Not to forget those who have showered me with kindness and made my life comfortable. God bless you. My gratitude also goes to Dele Ojutiku, Mr Egbetola, Abie Kamara-Taylor, Mrs Mamley Bampoe, Theophosa Mona-Moke, Pastor Kofo Laseinde and Maria Nonxoloba.

To my special friends, Aruere Harriet Bukata, Lady Anita Duckworth-Bradshaw, Jackie Oni, Dr Oluwatoyin Magbagbeola, Esther Jadesola Daniel, Professor Chris Ugolo and Apostle Ada Nwachukwu. You all uplift me and I am proud and grateful to know you.

To my awesome Saladmaster family for supporting me on a healthy cooking journey and special thanks to Mark Jones and Matthew Raymond.

Also, I would want to give my special thanks to the fantastic Speakers Are Leaders family for holding my hand and pushing me forward, especially Ash, Mahtab, Steve Frew, Nicky Oke and Aminu Ahmadu. Special thank you to the staff at the Critical Care Unit in Croydon University Hospital, Dr Carol Butriss and

the Liver Intensive Unit in King's College Hospital, London, particularly to Mr Krishna Menon, Dr. Georg Auzinger, Dr. Tasneem Pirani and Laura O'Duffy.

Also special thanks to all the doctors, nurses and all those who have contributed to bringing me back to life, including the London Ambulance Services.

Also to my diligent family doctors - Dr. Desmond Okpara, Dr. Bakare and Dr. Whyte for their continual support.

Many thanks to my church and club members especially:

Liberty Christian Ministries for their support and prayers, especially Dr. Kevin Kerr & Sandra Kerr OBE, Derin & Sophie Bepo.

Mirela Sula and the Global Woman Club, London

Igbo Catholic Community, Croydon, London

St Mary's Catholic Church, West Croydon

Aboh Union, United Kingdom, for their all-round support both in and out of hospital, especially

Phillipa Uju De Beneducci, Felicia Lawson, Mr Emma Opiah and Mrs Adesina.

Finally, a special thank you to my mentors, Harry Sardinas and Lily Patrascu, who have brought me to where I am today. I'm very grateful for coaching me and giving me a good reason to believe in myself. Also, thank you for your patience and encouragement to keep this book going when I was overwhelmed with all my hospital appointments. Your support is phenomenal. Thank You!

I am especially grateful to the incredible Segun Ogundimu, who religiously nursed me back to health, brushed my teeth in hospital and kept insisting that I finish a spoonful of mashed potatoes.

To my mother, Grace Ulo Onyekweli, who was my point of entry into this world, thank you for everything you did – you once carried me safely out of a burning hospital in Onitsha to save my life.

To my supportive brothers, Augustine, Dr Mathew, Christopher and Olisa Onyekweli.

And thank you to my beautiful sisters, Mrs Omogo Adiasor and Ms Evelyn Onyekweli, who stood by me during my time – more than one month – in a coma.

Thank you to Lily Patrascu with her Brand For Speakers programme, which helped me organise my ideas, coached me on my personal branding and helped me put this book together – and, as a result, made my dreams of becoming a published author come true.

I dedicate this book to my creator, who facilitated my recovery and continues to be my strength.

Dedication

I would like to dedicate this book to my inspiring and precious children, Damilola and Tosin

Ogundimu, who have come into my life to make it more meaningful.

They are my guardian angels and have saved my life on multiple occasions.

Their zest for life made this book possible. My thoughts and reasoning for this book were to make your days easier as you become adults. Teach the skills in this book to your children so that they will become well-grounded.

I had no such guides for myself and as a result I struggled in my adulthood.

They were the first familiar faces that I saw on the day I came out of a long coma. Their happy faces on that day gave me the courage to embrace the path to healing, thereby giving me the life that I have today.

Every Day Is A New Chance To

REINVENT

YOURSELF.

The Reinvention Mastery Programme

The Reinvention Mastery Programme is based on the **Miracle Golden Evening Ritual,** which I designed after I woke up from my coma. It dramatically improved my quality of life and positively impacted me and those around me. I hope you will feel inspired to use it as well, so that you can feel excited and inspired to live the life you really want to live. My mission, after having been in a coma, is to share this particular ritual with as many people as possible, because I know how heartbreaking it was for my children to see me in a coma and to have to say their goodbyes several times whilst I was attached to life support.

I also know that I had less than a 0.1% chance of survival and I survived both thanks to the mercy of God and also an immense determination to share my message to help you achieve your dreams.

I am certain you would benefit from this ritual because it is much more than that; it is a movement and a way of life. I would like to encourage you to feel alive in every moment of your life and come out of that routine that is holding you back in jobs you hate, piling up stress, worry, and overwhelming tasks.

I feel I was given a purpose in life and I had not accomplished it.

Luckily, I was given **a second chance,** but not everyone is that fortunate. So don't wait, get started today!

REINVENTION MASTERY PROGRAM

1. GRATITUDE
2. NUTRITION
3. FORGIVENESS
4. FAMILY
5. ENCOURAGEMENT
6. ACCEPTANCE
7. HELPFULNESS
8. RECONNECTION
9. TAKE CARE OF PLANTS
10. REST
11. SCHEDULE
12. PRAYER
13. ASKING FOR HELP
14. LISTENING
15. BE PRESENT
16. HAPPINESS
17. BE THE BEST VERSION OF YOURSELF
18. DON'T COMPARE TO OTHERS
19. SUPPORTIVE PEOPLE
20. IMPROVE YOURSELF
21. EXERCISE
22. POSITIVITY

<u>Here is what the system entails:</u>

Gratitude
Nutrition
Forgiveness
Family
Encouragement
Acceptance
Helpfulness
Reconnection
Taking Care Of Plants
Rest
Schedule
Prayer
Asking For Help
Listening
Being Present
Happiness
Being the Best Version Of Yourself
Don't Compare Yourself With Others
Supportive People
Improving Yourself
Exercise
Positivity

Having
GRATITUDE
Will Level Up Your
ATTITUDE.

Gratitude

1. Gratitude For Being Alive

I am grateful for being alive. Whilst I was in a coma I didn't know where I was. Regardless of what seemed to be a hallucination during my state of coma, I survived, and that's what matters most. Beyond words, I'm grateful I'm still here and I am able to write and inspire people.

I thank God every day for being alive.

2. Gratitude To God And The Universe

Before my accident I had forgotten to live my true purpose. During the coma I dreamt I had a conversation with God and the angels and they reminded me that I will be given another chance to prosper and help others. I thought my purpose was just to marry and have kids. Little did I know God had greater plans for me – to inspire people and to make a difference. I believe I came back from the coma in order to prosper. In my dream I was told not to overlook myself.

Be

THANKFUL

For What You Have, While Working For What You Want.

3. Be Grateful For Things In Your Life

There is so much to be overwhelmingly grateful for. The moment you open your eyes on a cold morning, with your blanket over you and your head nicely comforted on your favourite pillow as you wake up, reminds you of how beautiful it is to simply wake up to a new day. Not everyone is given the chance to live another day. Death is inevitable and it excuses no one. The mere fact that you're still alive is worth giving thanks for.

Be
GRATEFUL
For Your Struggle,

Otherwise You Won't Find Your
STRENGTH.

4. Be Grateful For Your Obstacles

Childbirth. I am grateful for my challenges and my obstacles because they made me who I am. I was labelled barren and told I would not be able to have kids, even if I tried, and was advised by my doctors to not even try. Even though I had no money, I went for IVF. Fortunately, I got pregnant the first time. I found that the challenging experiences I faced only made me stronger.

Jobs. I used to work for NatWest bank in IT support, and then with the local government ombudsman. Suddenly, my husband told me that I should stay home. Eventually, I also stopped working for Mary Kay Cosmetics. I feel blessed because although I thoroughly enjoyed working in all those jobs, I knew I was destined to do something else with my life.

Near-Death Experience. My near-death experience included five heart attacks in four days. Can you imagine that? The doctors could not resuscitate me and all my organs failed me. They found nine blood clots blocking my brain, heart and lungs. Despite the fact I have been through many surgeries, in intensive care and under body rehabilitation, I am grateful for this experience because I realise how privileged I am to spend time with my children, and I now take advantage of every second of my life. I no longer worry over small things; I forgive more – I appreciate every moment as if it was my last moment.

Becoming Homeless. Before the coma, I didn't get on well with my husband. Just before the heart attack, I was stressed and worried. I became homeless when I left my husband and that also made me feel rather useless and stressed. I felt like a failure. I am now aware that being homeless and fearing about security made me more determined to overcome any situation in my life.

The Only Thing You Need To Take From Your Past Are

LESSONS.

5. Gratitude In The Morning

When you express your gratitude the night before, and when you also do it the following morning, it helps you achieve a balanced day; it calms you and doesn't overwhelm you. You actually start enjoying life, and finding happiness on a daily basis. Trust the power of getting up from your sleep. It's a gift. It's one of the most gracious gifts there is. When you wake up, just thank God for waking you up.

6. Be Grateful For The Opportunities In Your Life

Ever since that happened to me, when I wake up in the morning – whether it's snowing, or it's very, very hot – I remain grateful for another opportunity to live an extra day. Any day above ground is a good day. I know people complain, saying, "Oh, it's so hot today," and, "Oh, it's so cold today," but I don't mind whatever sort of day it is because to me, any day is good, as long as I'm able to wake up. Because sometimes we forget that.

7. Appreciate Every Little Thing That Comes To You Because That Will Empower You To Receive More

Sometimes great opportunities lie in little things. Your mere existence is an opportunity to seize every single day. Do you know how many people have died? They don't even see the light of the nice, new day. They didn't get the chance to push through life and chase their dreams.

HAPPINESS
Is Found In
GRATEFULNESS

8.   Gratefulness Starts With You.

If you don't feel appreciated, perhaps it is time to appreciate the people and the things around you first. Your change of attitude will attract more of what you want in your life.

If you start to be grateful for what you have and what you are, you'll be able to help others feel grateful, too.
A lot of people feel the need to be happy and loved, yet they are caught up in a routine of unhappiness. Perhaps they feel unappreciated, maybe they feel they don't belong or they feel left out, they feel nobody cares about them, they want choice

freedom, time freedom, financial freedom, happiness and joy.

However, if they'd suffered what I have suffered, they'd realise that it doesn't matter if they wake up penniless and all their money in the bank has gone, or if they wake up and find out their car's been stolen – it doesn't matter.

If you are in a tough situation, be reminded that God will replace everything that was taken from you, if you have the kind of pact that I have with God. Everything is replaceable.
So, with that mindset, I don't lose things.
I only have gratitude towards things.

9.   Create A Daily Gratitude List

People usually forget the blessings and remember the struggles, instead. I used to have this kind of mindset before, and I'm grateful that I overcame it. My gratitude notebook kept me grounded.

Here's what you can do: you can have a gratitude notebook where you write down the things you're grateful for, daily. This will remind you during hard times that there are so many things you are grateful for, despite the difficulties you are facing. It will keep you strong. Having a gratitude list will help you remember how blessed you are.

Nutrition

1.   Minimise Your Coffee Intake

I'm one of those who loves to take a sip of an evening coffee, but I don't do it anymore. I no longer consume too much caffeine. It is important to watch your health, especially in your evening routine.

2.   Avoid Irregular Sleep

This is common to all and I admit I used to be guilty of this. Right now, I'm reducing my irregular or long daytime nap. I also optimised my bedroom environment, considering it reduces stress and helps me relax.

3.   Eat Healthy

I used to buy fast food and I didn't even used to bother watching my diet. I used to teach health, but I did not follow what I was teaching. I now have actually started practicing what I teach. I think it had to do with my mind. I changed my mindset and the way I think. I made a conscious choice to eat healthy. I started eating well – vegetables and salad. I don't rush my food anymore. I began to clear my mind and watch my diet carefully and stopped eating late at night.

Don't Let Your

PAST

Ruin Your

PRESENT.

Forgiveness

1. Forgive Yourself

You cannot forgive others if you don't forgive yourself first. Everything you do starts with you and how you handle the situation you are in. To forgive yourself, simply acknowledge that it's okay to make mistakes.

2. Forgive Those Around You

We stumble in so many ways. Nobody is perfect and we must acknowledge that. Some of us stumble accidentally, not intentionally.

Holding onto anger doesn't help you. Hence, it wraps you into resentment.
Forgiving will help you move on with life and start something new.

Forgiving those around you doesn't mean you are condoning their actions, nor does it mean they had the right to cause you pain. There are still going to be consequences they must face, but forgiving them releases you from the hurt. Always put it into your heart and mind that you have the power to forgive.

DON'T
Let Your
Past Have
Power
Over You.

3. Let Go Of Anger

Anger can cause stress. Even though I used to be stressed, I used to push it away, thinking I could overcome it. I thought I was a super woman. I didn't deal with my stress, but used to completely ignore it. Healing yourself from anger takes recognition that you've been hurt, but also acknowledging that you need to forgive yourself and others in order to move on with your life. Being stuck in anger has a corrosive effect on your health, both physically and emotionally.

Be patient. Don't let anger define you. Don't let it consume you.

Letting go of anger brings about transformation and revelation, as if a new person emerged from within. You are then a whole new person with a renewed perspective of what used to anger you.

Family

1. Reason For Living

I knew if I suddenly left this world, nobody would be there to look after my kids. It's one of the greatest reasons why I am still here today – my kids. Before my accident, I really struggled with my life. I did not feel like I had a voice. It's like I was just being dictated to by my environment and with my choices. Everyone said I should be this or should be that. I never felt really authentic or loved what I was doing. Nothing seemed to interest me anymore. Life no longer seemed to have its spark.

My accident was a blessing in disguise. It gave me a reason for living. My desire to live the life I always wanted grew even bigger. Things have changed, now. I feel there's a sense of urgency within me that I must achieve my dream.

You need to have a reason to live.

Seek your purpose.

Your ultimate reason to live is not an idea, it is life itself. It's the way you think and feel. Ask yourself these questions: "Why do I get up every day? What keeps me going?" Take your time as you ponder.

2. Check Three Things You Can Do With Your Family

Talk to your family every evening. I always try to talk to my children and my husband in the evening. Why? Because communication is the key to long-lasting and strong relationships. It's the foundation of trust in the family. It is also much easier to talk when you are not rushed.

I know you are probably busy with your day job. It consumes most of your time from morning until late afternoon. That's okay. You work to provide for your family and that's totally fine. It's great, actually. But despite your busy day, you must make time for your family. Before you go to bed, check with your kids, talk to your kids and/or your spouse. Ask them how their day was and if they're okay or not.

Be Present With Your Family. Ask your family what part of the day they liked best. Try to use that as a topic for conversation, praise them and make them feel special. Listen carefully and attentively to what they say and pay close attention to their body language, as well. If you notice something you would like them to change, tell them in a way that's not confrontational; for example, "You are very good at tidying your room, it's looking so nice. Can you try keeping it like that, so that you always enjoy your room?" As for you, share with them what made up your day, your highs and lows. Be open. Let them know your thoughts and feelings, and your plans for the next days to come. Again, communication is the key to long-lasting and healthy relationships.

Encourage your children to be open about their problems. If you have young children, you don't want them to grow up sharing their problems with other kids, right? But you would appreciate it if they were open with you. So, start now.

If you have teenagers, now is the best time to guide them, especially since it's common for teenagers to undergo an identity crisis. They're most vulnerable in their teen years, more than ever.

Time cannot be brought back. But you can always make the most of your time now with your family.

3. Put Your Children's Feelings First

When you are having a conversation with your kids, put their feelings first and try to think about how they feel by putting yourself in their position.

4.   Involve Your Kids In Your Activities

When you involve your children in your daily routine by doing tasks with them, it enables you to not only spend quality time together but also avoid the school run rush in the morning. Here's what you can do with them: tidy the kitchen together, or do chores around the house whilst keeping them entertained, or make jokes together. It also helps you avoid stressing in the morning.

5.   Prepare In The Evening For the Next Day

To avoid a stressful morning for you and your family, it's best to prepare in the evening for the next day.

Here's what you can do:
- Bring cereal and plates to the table so that it's all done for the next day.
- Bring the dining table into the living room. It is easier and it encourages more conversation.
- Prepare the clothes you need for the following day.

6. Teach Your Kids

Before I got into a coma, I sometimes used to judge my kids, thinking they're not doing this or that properly. I was comparing them to other kids and I was telling them other kids were doing better than them at school. I used to be too hard on them. But when I came out of the coma, I realised that my family needed me. What if I hadn't made it? They wouldn't have seen me ever again. It made me become more tolerant, more compassionate, and eventually I started getting closer to them and sharing great moments with them.

I couldn't share how I felt about my life with my children before the coma. I always thought they were too young, since they're not yet in their twenties. However, now I'm able to tell them things, such as how I was when I was young. I am now even telling them where I put my things. When they say: "Why are you telling us this?" I say, "In case anything happens to me." You never know what might happen, and at least they'll know where all my things are.

I'm beginning to plan for the unexpected, so that they know what to do if it happens.

Our children learn at school; however, the best learning they can experience at a young age must be from their parents. You can start slowly, by just asking them how their day went and, if there's something about what they said that reminded you of your younger days, then you can start sharing stories to relate to them. Every single moment of time you spend with your kids, listen attentively and be fully present, and you will realise they appreciate it a lot more than you can imagine.

Encouragement

1. Encourage Yourself

Who else would encourage you better than yourself? Direct words of encouragement and positivity towards yourself. Encourage yourself to speak positively about yourself.

One of the biggest things I discovered is that we wait for people to save us. Stop waiting to have someone save you. There is nobody who will save you but yourself. You have got to do it. When you take action, you can't see all the doors until you step up. You have to take action now. Even if it's only a small step.

2. Encourage Those Around You

Being able to sympathise doesn't only mean feeling the problem, but also encouraging others. If you have friends who are struggling and you know their situation, encourage them with positive language so that they feel they aren't alone.

Positive language has a tremendous impact on

others. Not only that, it also has a ripple effect of transformation on those around you.

Your friends and family sometimes feel discouraged to take action because they are afraid of being criticised or being judged.
By encouraging them to take small actions, they will feel motivated to do more.

3. Know That You Only Have One Life To Live

You only have one life to live and you can't trade your life with someone else's. When it gets taken, you won't be able to take it back. I would have just been history, but I am here because I'm determined to make a difference in this world.

Acceptance

1. Accept Yourself

I used to call myself stupid, but I realised that calling myself stupid won't help me. That's why I stopped calling myself stupid, and accepted everything about me. Therefore, you should not call yourself stupid anymore. God made you who you are for a reason. Your destiny lies in who you are, and what you're created for.

Embrace the real you.

Love the real you.
You are perfect and beautiful exactly the way you are.

2. Accept Others

Accept every single person without making any judgements. Once you learn to accept yourself, it equips you to be more considerate when dealing with other people without judging. Accepting others can give you peace of mind and a strong self-image.

3. No Resentment

I used to go to sleep filled with resentment. I used to tell my kids off, but now I am just grateful that my kids and my husband exist. My family banned him and I used to be angry with him. After waking up from my coma, I decided not to plant hatred in my heart.
I started to be patient with everything.
If my friends don't call me, I don't get upset.
I allow others to live.
It's normal for you to feel resentful at times, but

allowing that feeling to remain is a different thing. Instead of resenting and focusing on the problem, why don't you focus on the solution? It's a healthier way of dealing with resentment. You can also look twice at your analysis of the situation you are most resentful about. Maybe it's really not that big, maybe you are just holding resentment based on your perceived faults.

4. Acknowledge That Life Is Out Of Balance

Sometimes, the universe gives you this accident or that event in order for you to acknowledge that your life is out of balance. And, after years of following the same routine, you would love the opportunity to come out of the vicious circle, out of the rat race, and help other people to reinvent themselves, as well.
But reinvention is not possible when there's no acknowledgement of what you truly feel or what you truly are.

5. Acknowledge That You Are Not Alone

It's common for people who are struggling to

assume that they are alone. Perhaps, like you, there are others that at some point in their life feel lost, or they feel stressed, or they have a situation wherein they are just stuck in some way. Know that you are just one of the hundreds of thousands, and even millions, of people that are in a tough situation at some point or another.

When everything around you falls apart like an earthquake just struck you without notice, stand up and step out of the way; the world isn't ending for you yet. Rise up and go talk to your trusted friends and family.

Helpfulness

1. Be helpful with others

Be kind and friendly.

If we look everywhere, we become aware of how much substance and beauty people are able to generate.

Like kindness, helping is a gift that empowers the giver. Sometimes we receive help in return from those we assisted; even more often, our helpfulness flows through the world as other people freely pay it forward.

Money is a tool, not a means. By having money, you can use it to help others.

I can motivate and inspire you using the Miracle Day/ Golden Evening System in 90 minutes.

Find that particular thing in you that you can share with others. It doesn't have to be extravagant. You can start by asking yourself: "How am I living right now? What is my mission for the future?" Share with others how they can get out of whatever is affecting them adversely to create the transformation into happiness and creativity, and take a step towards creating their reality.

Reconnection

1. Rest

Take time to rest and reconnect with yourself and your desires. I now take a rest sometimes, to play with my children or to watch TV. I used to always be busy and preoccupied; I always used to feel angry with my children if they didn't respect 100% of what I was asking them to do. I have learnt to say, "no". I now say, "I am resting." Some people don't even come to see me anymore since I was in the coma.

2. Meditate

Meditation helps you to mentally clear all the negative thoughts and enlightens you to be emotionally calm. It's like doing a body scan and consciously relaxes your body from head to toe. Sometimes we just need to get away from the noise and stay still, to declutter our minds and fill it again with helpful thoughts.

How do I do it?

I think about what I am doing and I meditate at different times.

I reflect on what I did before and what's ahead.
The best time to meditate is early in the morning.
So, try it first thing tomorrow and see how it changes your entire day.

3. Look After Yourself

I look after myself. Before, I didn't used to bother taking care of myself. You can start by checking your body and not ignoring any symptoms. It only takes a few moments to go to your doctor for a check-up. Better to be ready for anything, and treat it before it gets worse.

4.   Be Sensitive To Your Inner Being

Have you ever had that feeling wherein there's something inside of you? It's like there's a voice in your head that keeps saying that you have to do something and it repeats: "Do it now, do it now."
It is reminding you that this is the right time.
I now feel this is the right time for me. I feel as if I am guided by instructions on what to do, and on how to create the system to use to reinvent myself to be more confident and help myself and other

people to prosper.

The very thing that helped me recover is not my own thoughts, but my belief in the divine grace. I believed in it because it was given to me when I was in the coma, and that helped me to trust in what has been given to me. And that is what I use in helping people. Faith helps you stay on track.

5. Do Something You Love

In order for you to live the life you want, you must be carefree, happy, peaceful on the outside, and have that unexplainable peace within. While I was in a coma, I went to different places; I went visiting all over the world in one day. I went to South Africa, South America, everywhere, as if my bed was tied to an aeroplane.

What I wanted to say is – do what you love while you still can. Do not wait for the day when everything will just stay as a dream. Do it while you can. Not later, not next time, but now.

Do something small or big for yourself, before it is too late. Wear your favourite perfume, smell the roses, bake instead of buying cakes, do anything you adore for yourself – a massage, a pedicure, a new haircut. You need to feel loved so you can share even more with the world. And it all starts with loving yourself and appreciating yourself.

6.   Communicate What You Really Want, Without Blaming, While Taking Responsibility

The root cause of all misunderstandings is lack of clear communication. Oftentimes, we can't clearly say what we want. Rather, we beat around the bush.

Be honest about what you feel.

Withholding what you feel creates distance and perhaps disconnection with the people around you. If you're upset with someone, let that person know.

7.   Sit Down And Think About What You Are Doing

Think about what you're currently doing, and ask yourself if it's worth sacrificing your life for your daily routine.

If you're having a problem with your job, if the one you are working at doesn't give you satisfaction, then look for a different type of job that will.

8.   Rebalance

Take the time to disconnect from the phone, the routine, your everyday issues, and take the time to reflect in order to keep a healthy balance between mind, body and spirit. Think about what you're going to do for the day, and check whether your body feels right. Your body is continuously sending you signals about the right direction to take. However, many times you might simply be too busy to listen to these signals.

Take the time to rebalance the body because otherwise there may come a time when you will become too drained and exhausted to be able to function properly.

One of the ways to rebalance yourself is to draw a circle and divide it into segments – make one for each of the main areas of your life, such as family, self-care, work, and spiritual. You can also add any other area that is important to you – creativity, dance, fun, etc. Use it as a guide to how to spend your day.

Basically, it means you do one thing for yourself, one for the family, one for work, and one for your spirit, as well as paying attention to any other areas that are of importance to you. Commit to yourself that every morning, when you wake up, instead of jumping out of bed and checking your phone, you will just spend five minutes, or even ten, thinking about yourself. You don't have to meditate, but if you want to meditate that's fine. Actually, it's better. Writing down what you need to do the next day with those four (or more) aspects in mind will help you balance your day.

Take Care Of Plants

1. Water The Flowers

Taking care of your environment will bring more love back to you. Just like us humans, flowers are here to share life. We should take care of God's creation. There are a few things you can do, such as arranging flowers and talking to them for five or ten minutes.

2. Speak To Nature

I now appreciate what I have much, much more. When I see nature and the things around me, I'm more appreciative than ever. When I see a tree, I speak to the tree and I thank it, for it has been there for perhaps hundreds of years. It has seen a lot, been through a lot, but it is still standing, despite the test of time.

Schedule

1.   Stay Committed To What You Have Promised

Before my accident, I didn't used to schedule things that I had to do. I used to procrastinate and cancel appointments at the last second. Right now, I am more committed to what I have promised to do. That makes me feel better about my achievements and helps other people to appreciate me more.

2. Assess What You Did During The Day

Having a checklist or a "to-do" list helps you to be more organised. Actually, during my meditation I always assess how am I doing today and make sure that I am now much better, more productive, and much healthier than yesterday.

3. Plan For Tomorrow

Write down three important things that you have to do the next day. You need to start writing it in the evening, at least by the time you go to bed.

When you wake the following day, you are not rushing around thinking of what you need to do.

So basically, write everything in the evening as you put things away.

Well, you don't need to write absolutely everything, because we don't want to overwhelm ourselves. Remember, we're trying to take it nice and easy. Write the most essential things that need to be done.

4. Acknowledge Yourself For What You Achieved

You can achieve three important things every day. If you plan in advance, you will find out that it's not so difficult. It's not overwhelming.

Before, I used to suffer from being overwhelmed and so I did not achieve what I wanted to. Everything used to be so difficult and I was getting stressed easily.

Now, I give myself credit for what I have achieved.

5. Tick Off The Goals Achieved

You have a list, right? So, once you've completed something, tick it off your list to avoid repetition of tasks. It will give you a great sense of achievement and also ease your burden, one tick at a time.

6. Leave The Ones You Didn't Achieve Out For Another Day

There's no need to rush things through, because all you have to do is to focus on what is really important. If there's anything you weren't able to finish today, then do it tomorrow. Be gentle with yourself and be reminded that everything has its perfect timing.

7. Try To Delegate Some Goals For Tomorrow

You should check on your goals list and identify what areas you would like to get done today.

It is best to get the essential tasks done and leave less unimportant ones for later, rather than get overwhelmed and suffer with stress because of it.

Prayer

When you wake up in the morning, it's good to pray.
Pray and feel gratitude for being alive today.

"Thank you for me not having a panic attack today.
Thank you for me waking up today.
Thank you for my being able to live today.
Thank you for giving me another chance to see the kids today."

I used to be stressed about sleeping without getting 100% of my tasks done. Now, I let things go. I remind myself that tomorrow is another day.

Sometimes I feel God is talking to me, reminding me: "Have you started doing XYZ?"

1. Prayer Of Forgiveness

For a few years, I was struggling to have children. My husband said we could just adopt.

However, I had a strong feeling I was going to be blessed with the miracle of having children. Whilst in Africa, I had had four abortions and now I thought God was punishing me.

I was ready to adopt, but then I started praying.
I prayed and asked for forgiveness for doing things without thinking. And so, after three years, we got another child. If you miss one opportunity, sometimes another one appears.

2.   Prayer Of Gratitude

One of the things I incorporate in my prayers is thanking God on a daily basis. I think it is important to thank God that you're awake.

Don't wake up in the morning and just go through your phone, and be checking who sent you a message on WhatsApp.

Just wake up and thank God that you're awake. Doing that has helped me to keep myself grounded, and I also teach that as part of my package.

I show people how to look for things to be grateful for, instead of focusing on things that are not there. Also, to focus on how to actually look for what you can thank God for.

3. Trust In God

I want you to know you are blessed and you should continue to have hope, even in your darkest place, because obstacles are only there to make us stronger and to enable us to become better people. Know that you're blessed to have come to this earth to make a difference. You will find your own purpose just by trusting in God, and by trusting yourself, too.

And what message are you sending people with your actions? Try to ponder on this.

<u>Asking For Help</u>

1.   Ask For Help When You Need It

I used to feel terrible every single day because I was overcome by guilt. In the lead up to the accident, I was depressed and stressed.

I felt guilty for having problems with my husband. My daughter got sick and I was blaming myself, and my partner was also blaming me.

I felt guilty for having had the four abortions. My husband got arthritis and he could not walk for a year.

He didn't understand what was happening, and he allowed alcohol to affect his judgements.

He used to frequently phone the police on me and wanted custody of the kids.

He now makes an effort.

I used to do everything myself.

I was overworking myself mentally before, but now I share everything with him.

The reality is that you don't have to face huge tasks alone. Find someone whom you can talk to or share the burden with. We need other people's help from time to time to keep ourselves keep sane and avoid getting overwhelmed with stress.

Listening

1. Be Fully Present

Listen better, focus and be fully present with the person in front of you. Show the person talking that you want to hear them. Look at them and respond when needed. Remove any distractions, such as looking at your phone, checking your email or fixing your things. Listen to understand what the person is talking about, rather than just waiting for your turn to respond.

2. Listen Attentively

You have to listen carefully to people and anticipate what's going to come. You always have to pay attention to what the other person is telling you. The thing is that not all people in your life can influence you to go unto the right path. It's just that you have to collect all the good things that are coming from them and relate it to your own life, then evolve from it.

LEARN

From Your Past And

CHANGE

Your Future.

Happiness

1. Remove Resentfulness

I used to be resentful, but my life transformed after the coma. I now feel much happier without doing anything in particular. One way to be happy is to start thinking positively and remove your resentment from your past. Do not wait for an accident to strike you before changing – begin today to create the life you want to live.

2.   Do What Makes You Happy

Not doing the things that make you happy will result in you losing your life's purpose. Imagine turning forty-five years old, then finding you're burned out or angry that you've wasted all your life working for somebody else, making millions for them, but your whole life is now a mess.

You may have some money, but you're not happy. Perhaps you are tired of not doing what you really love or are passionate about.

Perhaps you feel you have wasted your time, your effort, sleepless nights, sacrificing time you could have spent with your family, perhaps you have not been present for your friends.

Consider doing one little thing that gives you pleasure or makes you happy or gives you joy.

If You're Going To Reinvent Yourself, Make Sure To

BE THE

BEST

VERSION

OF YOU.

Be The Best Version Of Yourself, Don't Compare With Others

1.   Have The Right Attitude

Social media can put you under a lot of pressure to be in the limelight. Other people may seem to be doing so well in comparison to you.

Perhaps you may want recognition or you simply want to feel loved and get approval. Perhaps you want to show your peers you "made it", or perhaps you want to show that you are successful. You may hide away if you feel you aren't as good as your peers in any way. You may look at Facebook and say, "What about me? When am **I** going to be successful?" That gives you a bad attitude, because you aren't happy.

It's important to remember that you don't need to compare yourself with others. The only person to compare yourself with is yourself. Are you a better person compared to who you were yesterday? if the answer is yes, simply remember the key to happiness is making progress. I have always been a happy person, so I want to influence the people around me to have the same mentality.

2.   Be Brave

If you are afraid of living life without achieving your desires and dreams, or if you are afraid of not being able to make a difference in life, I understand – I used to feel exactly the same way.

I used to feel the need to prove myself to my family. I felt I was going to be an international speaker.
People were going to listen to *every word* I said. People would clap loudly and admire me.

The reality was quite stark: nobody believed I could do it. Not my family or those around me. **Not even me**. I felt there was a huge contradiction in me: I felt that I was born with a purpose to do something, and I didn't fulfil that purpose. I was dragging my feet most days. I didn't see my purpose.

I didn't want to live because every day felt like a nightmare. My body was showing signs of overwhelm. I was trying to ignore all the signs.
And I did, right up until the Universe sent me the biggest sign nobody could ignore – the heart attacks. I suffered for a full year after the coma

and, even though I am still undergoing multiple surgeries, continuous body rehabilitation, strict medication, and I am continuously on the doctors' watch list, I feel joy in every single moment because I now know the power of being alive.

I am so grateful for being able to spend time with my children.

Whilst in the coma, the instruction that was given to me in my dream was that I have to come back and try to pass on the message to people.

I was instructed to come back to prosper, because we've all been put on Earth to fulfil a purpose. So, if you find that you are poor, you may not actually be poor in all aspects. You might be poor financially, but you could be rich in other ways. It's your job to find what you can leave as a legacy.

It doesn't matter what that is.

It's up to you, as long as it helps others.

I've come back to use my talents and skills to help others, so that they can be prosperous, as I'm prospering now. And I challenge you to do the same.

BE WHO YOU'VE ALWAYS WANTED TO BE.

Improve Yourself

1.　Keep Yourself Beautiful

Look after yourself.

Take your make-up off and take care of yourself.

Go out on a shopping spree and buy your favourite dress. Pamper yourself by going to a spa for a body scrub, facial and nail makeover.

Reward yourself for being you, for being this beautiful person, not just outside, but also on the inside.

2.   Worry Less

Take time out and don't worry so much.
Things will then just fall into the right place. You don't have to rush things. Good things come to those who take action consistently on the essential critical factors. I am now proud to be able to inspire and help others who went through the same situation I did.

3.   Create Your Own Journal And To-Do List

Learn to create a system for your day, otherwise you may feel depressed. I always keep a notebook by my side. I write down three things I want to do when I wake up tomorrow.

You can do this, too.

Write your tasks before midnight.

For example: I am going to make two calls. Write the name of the person and their phone number; make things easy for yourself. Focus on doing three important things each day.

I created a journal called the Reinvention Mastery Journal that will be released soon, as a complement to this book.

WHAT HAPPENED YESTERDAY DOESN'T MATTER NOW.

Today Is Another Chance To Reinvent Yourself.

4.   Live In The Moment.

Living in the moment means being present with all your senses. The very reason why I couldn't live in the moment, before, used to be my procrastinating attitude – I was always late for appointments.

I used to do things last minute and that used to hinder me from enjoying moments in life, because I had to work on something that was due.

Prior to my change of mindset, I had this strong inclination to persevere, yet I had no courage to do so. Now, I am more determined to take each day seriously and manage my time wisely.

5.   Take Control Of Your Life

As you come across many obstacles, you have a choice to either give up and be a victim or become stronger and use the obstacle as an opportunity to grow.

You may struggle with negative thoughts, and that can hinder you in having full control over your life.

You might be thinking you have no choice and you can't do anything. But when you choose to be powerful and extraordinary, you manage to surpass any obstacle and any situation.

Life is simpler when you focus on what's important to you. And that might be just to be there for your kids, to share your message with people, to put your one foot in front of the other, to recreate and reinvent yourself. And for that, you are very inspiring, for your children first of all, and for the world as well.

I think that by doing what you're doing now, just by speaking and by sharing your message, you could be inspiring someone that is currently depressed or those who currently feel like they're stuck in a rut. And, you know, seeing your story could help them to get inspired. You could save thousands of lives, not just one.

Stop Finding Yourself, START CREATING YOURSELF.

6. Reinvent Yourself

Imagine a new you.

There is no limit to what you can be, do and have, as long as you take action on the critical success factors that will drive you to success.

It took me a full year of painful body rehabilitation. I had to relearn everything, as I had forgotten pretty much everything I knew before the coma.

I'm already able to think coherently.

Remember, I was brain dead for almost a month.

Now, I can think properly again, though I still have some things I'm dealing with.

In terms of reinventing yourself and moving forward, I'm working on relearning words little by little, and I think that is more authentic.

Now, I can help myself and others better, since I am focusing more powerfully on the right things.

I finally know how to help different people, because I saw people that committed suicide in my dream, and I saw people that were depressed.

Now, I know how to talk to each and every one, so that they can change and then probably look at life differently.

To tell you honestly, a lot of people have benefited from what I've been sharing around my experience. People come to talk to me; they bring their children or parents.

I've been doing private talks with them, but I realised that this problem is widespread, which made me think that maybe it's better to let people know me, so they would know who to go to, to ask for help.

If more people know me, then they can benefit and they will be able to help their loved ones, as well.

That is why I decided to use this programme to help, instead of keeping it to myself and my family, and my friends, who are already benefiting from it.

7.   Focus On What's Important

I used to be a high-flyer, chasing money and career ascension. I used to work in an investment bank and I've worked before in the IT industry.
And then, when I awoke from the coma, I realised that where I worked meant nothing.

Because I had just boarded the same train that everybody's travelling on.

I'd say that the people that my programme would most benefit are the high-flyers, businessmen and businesswomen who spend all their lives making money.

It is also for you, if you are continuously working hard but you are not taking the time to listen to your body, and you are denying your body and soul the need to relax, recharge and refuel with the energy required in order to become even more productive and more vibrant.

You're making money, but are you looking after what is really important?

If that person is you, I would refocus on what you are truly passionate about and what brings you joy in your life.

I'm not saying don't make the money, you can make the money, but make sure that you're focusing on the right things, as well – your family, your personal happiness, taking enough rest.

8.   Conduct An Inventory Of Your Life

One of the things I would like you to do is to book yourself on a retreat and conduct an inventory of your life.

I know most of you spend your time looking after your children, or working, and you forget about taking care of yourself and your partner.

Sometimes, when the kids have flown out of the nest, when they have gone to university or they're all married and settled in their own homes, you find yourself with just your spouse.

And you realise, it's like you're strangers.

Yes, strangers, because you haven't taken the time to pay attention to what's happening with your life or theirs. You may have forgotten to take care of your spouse's needs, or forgotten to make him or her feel special. You have forgotten to take inventory.

Your spouse fell in love with you years ago because she or he realised how special you are; however, after a while, you may have forgotten to show your partner how much you care. Your partner is now just someone who is always part of the landscape – until your partner is no longer there and you can't fathom how it happened.

Take every moment to make your partner feel special. You also won't know how you are doing until you regularly take the time to retreat and channel your energy again into your relationships, your family and your friends.

It's actually like when you are doing your New Year's resolution – take an inventory and find out where you are.

Because when you do that, it's easier for you to know what is working and what is not working.

Otherwise, you'll just be carrying on the same as before.

9.   Make A Change

Every year, you have to change what you do. What worked for you this year might not work for you next year. So, you have to change and, sometimes, you have to throw something away – at least, if doing that is for the better. Because it is not about your New Year's resolutions, it's not about having bigger TV sets, or having better cars, and buying signature clothes.

You know what's it about? It's all about yourself. It's all about you and your partner sitting down together to make your relationship better and more meaningful throughout the year. You must be the source of your change, especially when it's between you and your partner. Change is not about changing who you are, it is about changing what you think is not working anymore for you and your partner.

Don't try changing him or her.

Change yourself.

And, by changing yourself, there might be a change in your daily routine and your partner might notice it.

Keep your partner entertained by varying the activities you two get to do together – whether that is watching a musical together, a movie, cooking a nice meal together, or whatever else you both enjoy. Regardless of whether you have children or not, you need some alone time to reconnect with each other and bring back that feeling you had at the beginning of the relationship.

As for your friends, they must be your supporters, so you can be a better person. What they want to be must not dictate who you should be. It is okay to go out and hang out with them, but never forget who you are and what you want.

Reinvent yourself by first taking stock of who you are, then defining who you want to be; after that, you can make a gap analysis so you can understand the change that is desirable. That will help you understand what kind of suggestions you should accept so you, too, can transform yourself and your future.

It is possible to achieve all these changes in life, because knowing your priority and taking the important matters seriously will help you have a vision of who you want to be in the year to come. Time management is the key to having a wonderful year. By focusing on priorities and positives, and managing your time, you can achieve a step-by-step change in yourself.

10. Leave A Legacy

I am a transformational coach and I believe that I'm here both to show you the way and also to help you in your transformation of becoming a better version of yourself and the legacy you'll eventually leave.

I know I've got my children and I can leave a legacy for them.

But I want to leave a legacy that will help a lot of people, not just my immediate family.

I want to leave a legacy that will help women, so that they can also leave a legacy, in turn.

You see, if it's just me changing one person, or myself and my family, it's not going to be big.

I want everybody to benefit, so that it will be like a ripple effect for helping the world, so that you learn from me and pass it on to your family, or to your friends.

And I will share with you what I've learned, because not everybody is going to go into a coma to learn, like I did.

I mean, I wouldn't say I've been fortunate to have experienced being in a coma as I don't think it's a good thing to have suffered five heart attacks.

But then, I was able to go there to learn how to live a better, more fulfilling life.

11. **Being Positive Can Have An Impact On Others**

Being positive impacts others in more ways than you can imagine. Sometimes, all you need is someone to believe in you when you are doubting yourself, to give you that extra edge so you can achieve more than you ever believed possible. My actions speak for themselves. I am now much more committed to what I promise to do. If I say I'm showing up, I show up, and I'm also positive whilst there.

I'm positive no matter what happens, and I generally feel much better and I smile.

Because, when people see me, they don't know what to say.

They all go, "Oh, my God," when they see me making an effort to walk with my crutches or something, and they don't smile back.

So, after I show them hope, everything changes. That's what I do with my actions, regardless of how I feel – I show them that there's hope.

12. How To Leverage

I want to create helpful programmes so you can leverage my experience and not have to go through the same thing I did. I will conduct and organise workshops that will address certain issues you may have experienced that have made you doubt yourself or that have kept you out of balance.

My intention is to create a transformation in you, so you are able to be happy and feel less stressed and be more focused.

The message I would like to share is that if you can recover from such a serious illness, then you can also use whatever life throws at you in a positive way.

When you get your act together and you are aligned in your actions, your body, your mind, your spirit and your soul, it's easy for the money to follow.

Because if you don't get your act right, even if you are making a hundred thousand a year, you're going to waste it.

When you are focusing only on making money, but you are not feeding yourself well or taking time to reflect, when you are not checking with yourself, and you're not organising your life in a positive way, your body starts running on empty – it is drained of energy and it is drained of life.

When you are not aligned with your general tasks, you may make a lot of money or a little, but you will struggle to keep it; you may waste it, or you may just give it away. What may happen is also that you may struggle to focus on your daily tasks or perhaps not see the meaning of it all and feel lost.

How many people do you know or have you seen that kill themselves, despite apparently having everything a normal person might desire – such as a loving family, a loving spouse, enough money in the bank to live any kind of lifestyle, a gorgeous body, a caring group of friends and even millions of adoring fans?

These people have lost the will to live and that is because perhaps they forgot to take the time to reflect and create the lifestyle they needed for themselves.

They forgot to love themselves and appreciate themselves.

I think that's really important, because if you make a lot of money, but you're not happy, you will not be able to feel fulfilled and attract abundance in your life. When you feel sad or depressed, you repel the people you need in your life. Negativity attracts more negative people. I don't see even see the point of doing that.

I think it's really important to be happy, to be positive, to be excited, just living and savouring life.

You can start attracting or creating the life that you want by taking small steps to start over and set up new ways to achieve your goals in life.

13.   Creating The Life You Want

You can restart your life with a mindset of gratitude.

Gratitude means being thankful that you're still here on Earth and you have a wonderful purpose.

It's always a joy to reminisce about good times in life and one of the best ways to remind yourself is to write about them.

Try and write down things in your thoughts.

You may not like writing, but try to write a word or two that could help you remember.

It helps you to be organized and focused.

It's not easy to achieve that, but just by simple exercise or by following certain programmes, you'll find yourself able to do that.

And, before you know it, it becomes something you can do.

14. Daily Habits/Routines

It is important to create daily habits of getting things done. I used to promise myself that I would write my to-do list, dust the TV, put this or that in my diary. I don't do that anymore.

If I have a few small tasks that can be done and got out of the way in a few minutes, I just go and do them.

I don't do that for everything, but I try to just be more productive. I try to take action instead of just planning. Before, I was a planner, but I was not taking any action.

So now, I do more actions than planning.

It is still a good idea to have a plan, but if there's something you can do right now, just do it.

15.   Be A Blessing To Others

My life before used to be so out of order. I was not even sure what I was doing. I was just getting by, most days.

I was a contributor for others. I contributed and spent a big amount of money for charities.

I didn't have a lot, but I was helping people and individuals.

If I could see somebody suffering, I automatically would help them in any ways I could.

I thought that was very silly, because I was also struggling myself.

I realized what I did was not just contributing to those people but contributing to life itself.

I was actually helping my own spirit, by being there for people when they had problems.

Anybody that knew me would say, "Adaobi will help you if you have any kind of problems."

Every time I helped others, I felt that the Universe was helping me, in return.

I felt God's hands lifting my burdens in exchange for me having helped others.

You can start by being sensitive to the needs of the people around you. It doesn't have to be a huge help, it can simply be listening to your friend who's struggling or just being there for him/her.

16.   **Power/Karma Of Doing Good**

I believe in the power of doing good.

When I was in the coma, I was told by the angel, "Even if you are doing good for others, you also have to take care of yourself." For instance, if you have a bowl of rice and you see somebody that hasn't eaten, you don't just give them all the bowl.

If you're hungry, pour some rice for yourself. Take a little bit for yourself, and give the rest.

Before, I used to give all the bowl of rice away, and keep nothing for myself.

Then I started feeling resentful because I had nothing left. I don't think that's smart.

I hope you won't experience the same thing I did.

You have to learn to look after yourself, as well. It's true when people say, "You cannot help others if you don't know how to help yourself." Remember that you are giving yourself to people, and for you to be able to do that, you have to be whole, you need to have something to give. Constantly giving without receiving can drain you. You need to keep enough for yourself for you to be able to help others as well.

Practice self-care – you have to keep it balanced.

You can help, but also remember to help yourself, and your family.

17. **There's A Second Chance In Life**

My children would've been orphans if God hadn't given me a second chance in life. While I was in the coma, no one was taking care of my children. Thankfully, a family member showed up or else my children would've been taken to a foster care home that would eventually have separated them.

There was a time when I came home after the coma and my children were so worried. They came to me while I was sleeping and said, "Mummy, Mummy, are you awake?"
They were trying to find out if I was still alive.
So, when I coughed they came running. They were told to come to the hospital and they heard that my life support would be turned off and that had a shocking impact on them.
When I was in hospital, my kids weren't allowed to see me. The people who took care of me didn't want my children to see me swollen.
I was black and swollen and the doctors didn't want to frighten my children.

The moment I came back home alive, my children became much happier. They started to tell me stories about their school and their homework.

My mother is happy that I'm alive. I saw her clearly when I was in the coma. She was sitting right next to me, even if she didn't come to the hospital. I could see her spirit. She was with me in spirit.
Now everybody is happy that I'm back.

Come to think of it, you only have one life to live. And, if you're lucky, a second chance in life after a near-death experience. So why don't you make the most of it? You can start by listing what you're passionate about and start doing those things one item at a time. I made a list for myself. You can, too, and maybe we'll have similar passions.

What Are You Passionate About?
Make a huge list of things, activities, people that bring you joy. For me these are some of the activities that make me happy:

- Helping people
- Music
- Nature
- Walking
- Talking
- Perfume
- Flowers
- Baking
- Children

- Books and self-help books
- Books about natural medicine
- Succeeding in something
- Having my own book
- Lipstick
- Driving
- Beautiful houses
- Bedsheets
- Cooking
- Creating
- Being imaginative
- Drawings

You can have a long list such as this one or make your own format that suits your style – it doesn't matter, just as long as it helps you. Add at least one thing that brings you joy to your planner of things to be done during the day.

Even better, include things that bring you joy in every activity – whether it is having a giggle, putting a smile on your customers' faces, making jokes, doing a dance during your break. I take any opportunity to have fun and I include it in my day. What fun diverse activities could you do whilst at work? Keeping entertained makes you feel like you aren't working, so it makes you much more focused and productive.

18.   **Mentor Or Coach**

Look for a coach and pay someone to help you rediscover yourself. If you follow what you have always done, you may never reach your potential and sometimes you can't achieve what you want at all.

Look for a mentor who has taken your same journey or can influence you; look for help from him or her. Look for someone that will point you in the right direction or who can help you discover yourself. Getting advice from a coach can save you time, money and effort, and the reality is that nobody can give you more time. You can buy any other thing, but time cannot be bought.

When I was in the coma, I saw my entire life flash before me.

The angel of the Lord came to me. I could hardly see his face since it was covered with light. The angel asked how my life was. I had to tell the angel what happened and he said, "No, no, no, that is not why you were sent there."

Right after, the angel taught me how to go back and put my life in order, and also live in a way that will make me happy.

I was tutored on how to live a better life.

I got the message from the Almighty.

After all that happened to me, I never thought I could get off my bed. Now I have a better understanding of the life I live. I gained knowledge about how to apply what I learned in life and during the coma, too.

When I woke up from my coma, I wrote down what I remembered.

I didn't even know if it was going to work, but I started practicing it.

It hasn't been a year since I woke up. I was discharged around the end of February 2018 and I can already see some progress.

19. Engage In Positive Conversation

Engaging in positive conversation is both therapeutic and encouraging. It gives you a sense of healthy connectivity to everything and everyone around you.

In my case, I enjoy talking with people, especially my husband. He is ready to talk when you ask the right question without arguments. Positive conversation involves a listening ear and an open heart. You must be in a good frame of mind.

In addition, when you engage with people, try to be less nosy. Some people are private and they won't open up just that easily. They might think you are trying to find out what they're doing if you ask too much. It might lead them to stay away from you and I bet you don't want that.

Exercise

1. Make Time For Exercise

Family bonding varies. There are days where exercise becomes a "thing" for me and my family. On days when the weather is nice, my family enjoys a walk or bike rides with the children.

If your family is involved in that very active phase of bringing up your children, your exercise break between work and child responsibilities will likely help you be calmer and more capable parents.

Surround Yourself With:

1. Supportive People

We need to help others to achieve their goals, because this is what we're meant to do here. The people that surround you could either make or break you. You must surround yourself with people who see the best in you. Surround yourself with those that lift you up, not put you down. Genuine support comes from a sincere heart. I know it won't be hard for you to identify these people. Once you're sure about them, invest your time, effort and

resources in them.
Invest in the right soil.
Why? Because you know they would someday do the same for you.

2. Successful People

If you surround yourself with successful people, you'll become successful, too. It's as cliched as it gets, but there's a popular saying that goes, "Tell me who your friends are and I will tell you who you are." Be around people who are already producing

the result that you want.
You can get helpful tips from them on how they became who they are now. Hard work pays off and I'm sure they also have their fair share of behind-the-scenes stories. Listening to them will begin to reconfigure your brain to their ideas and the principles they teach. The more you acquaint yourself with successful people, the more you learn and apply their knowledge, the easier it gets to do so.

3. Positive People

I used to be a grumpy person. I used to complain

about everything. I used to complain a lot about the weather, Brexit, and almost everything that's present at the moment. Thanks to my life-changing experience, I'm now optimistic about everything.

It's not easy to be positive when life throws stones at you. Without those positive people around me that reminded and encouraged me to push through with life, I would've remained grumpy.

Achievement

1.   Write Down Three Things You Want To Achieve

We've all had that moment where we just can't seem to muster the momentum to get things done. You might feel like you're getting things organized by creating a long to-do list. Frankly speaking, a long to-do list often leads to not getting things done. It acts as a demotivator, rather than a motivator. Oftentimes, seeing a long list causes panic. It builds up hesitation and doubt. Instead, write down only three things that you want to achieve in a day. For a start, it's a great way to begin assessing your achievement for the next twenty-four hours. This will help you stay on track with your objectives for the day.

You need to create your list the night before you plan to do the things on it. Why? So that you won't lie awake thinking about what you need to do the next day. Writing it down will allow your mind to relax, resulting in you getting enough rest to be effective and efficient the next day.

2. Write Down Two Key Things You Want To Achieve For Your Family Life

A strong family helps you keep life in order. In today's busy world, it's difficult for families to come together and spend time. Families nowadays rarely share a meal together due to differences in schedule.

If you are experiencing this, then it's high time for you to stop and do something about it.

Take some time and write down in your journal two key things you can do with your family. It could be as simple as eating dinner together once a week, or perhaps a two-day vacation – anything that could build up your relationship with them.

In conclusion, it's a wake-up call for you, and I feel like this is really the right moment for you to start sharing your message to thousands of people around the world in the same way.

It's high time for you who are reading to fulfil your full potential, to unlock your full potential, and to transform and reinvent your life in the same way that I have done.

Summary

Reinvent Yourself is a blueprint for you to succeed in your personal and business life.

It was created out of the struggles of a young mother who had lost her will to live. Her story is a reminder that the Universe will grant your command.

Adaobi's story is well-known by top surgeons and medical doctors around the world, as she shattered several medical records to still be alive. She's here, today, against all odds.

Having a very busy lifestyle and certain life challenges can be seen as burdens or as gifts. A cardiac arrest, heart attack or a diagnosis of heart disease is often a dramatic wake-up call for those that are lucky enough to survive such an event.

Adaobi would like you to see any obstacle or life-changing event as the gift that it is. It could be your deciding factor for creating a healthy lifestyle and a brand new you.

Some of us just live and do not really enjoy life.

Well, those days are over.

The reason for this book is to help you reconnect with your gifts, passions and what really makes you feel great.

It is a reminder that you are meant to discover the brilliance within and create infinite possibilities in your life.

Also, to remind you that looking after yourself first will make you a better person.

I have prepared a special masterclass for you as I would like to help you stay on track in your reinvention journey and also so that you can start practicing these tools I spoke about in the book.

Watch the FREE masterclass here: www.adaobionyekweli.com/masterclass

I would be most grateful if you could leave a review in amazon for me.
Hope to meet you someday!
You can subscribe to my social media channels:

Linkedin: Adaobi Onyekweli
Facebook: Adaobi Onyekweli
Youtube: Adaobi Onyekweli
Podcast: Reinvent Yourself Podcast

About The Author
Health Education – Accredited Trainer and Consultant

Adaobi is a reinvention coach, upcoming international speaker and author – founder of the Reinvention Mastery Programme.

Having suffered five heart attacks in four days, being declared brain dead and recovering more than one month later, Adaobi is an example of someone who recreated the story of her life from someone who wasn't living her true purpose to someone now dedicated to motivating clients who wish to adopt a new lifestyle to reinvent themselves, improve their health, fitness and appearance. Adaobi offers a realistic approach to attaining a healthy balance through nutrition.

She is the mother of two children and she is experienced in educational health, wellness, and nutrition. She has an impressive list of clients who enjoy her positive and empathetic attitude. Comfortable as a communicator, she designs customised programmes for clients to lose or gain weight, improve stamina and flexibility, and increase strength. Her excellent communication, counselling and persuasive skills, combined with her knowledge in health, nutrition and fitness issues, ensures that clients soon see an improvement in their physical and fitness endurance levels.

Prior to specialising in health education, Adaobi consulted to various prestigious organisations, through SHL, and worked at J.P. Morgan and Dresdner Kleinwort Benson.

Her role was to proactively interface with traders on the trading floor to ensure that data and the activities of those involved in dealing stocks and shares meshed in a smooth manner. These finely honed skills have been useful in designing fitness programmes for her current clients.

She later took her skills to facilitate the change from PEP to ISA in NatWest Bank and, later still, managed the information technology customer-facing aspect for the local government ombudsman in Victoria.

Her knowledge of health-related diseases or disorders, and suitable remedial measures, means that clients from around the world use her services and recommend her to others. Her knowledge of the latest trends in health care and the vital importance of cookware in maintaining health is unparalleled and much sought-after. Her diagnostic skills have been requested and used by medical doctors, and in both allopathic and holistic settings. Adaobi evolved her communication skills further, based partly on her earlier experience as a beauty consultant catering to the needs of clients who wanted to improve their body image. An advocate of lifelong learning, she took her Certificate of Mastering Sales and Influence in order to increase her ability to market her brand. She is a talented and generous trainer and consultant.

She believes that when you fully come alive as a person or through fulfilling your potential is when the people you're meant to serve feel magnetically drawn to you and pay you handsomely to transform their lives, regardless of how many followers you have.

And, most importantly, that's when you can start to have it all – the family, the lifestyle, the freedom, the legacy.

If you want to learn how to create a movement around your message, your life and your legacy, then this book is for you.

Spice up your next conference or events by partnering with the Miracle Lady, as she is popularly known. Her story is very profound and has been impacting very many people. Everyone that hears this lady speak undergoes a profound change in their life.

She survived a near-fatal crisis thanks to a series of miracles and the world-class care at King's College Hospital, Denmark Hill, London, United Kingdom.

Now, she wants to show you how you can redefine your life and create an environment that is rich with vibrancy and love, and has a positive impact on humanity and the planet.

44061189R00101

Printed in Poland
by Amazon Fulfillment
Poland Sp. z o.o., Wrocław